CODE

The Adventure Begins

Emma Lynch • Jon Stuart

Contents

OXFORD
UNIVERSITY PRESS

Welcome to Micro World!

Micro World zones

 Bugtastic

 Galactic Orbit

 Dragon Quest

 Wild Rides

 Jungle Trail

 Shark Dive

 Fiendish Falls

 Big Freeze

 Castle Kingdom

 Forbidden Valley

 Wonders of the World

 Pyramid Peril

 Marvel Towers

 CODE Control

Staff only

Meet Macro Marvel, inventor of Micro World!

Macro Marvel wants to build a Micro World in every town and city!

Macro Marvel
(billionaire inventor)

Meet Mini Marvel

Mini Marvel (age 8) is Macro's daughter. Micro World was her idea!

Mini Marvel
(Macro's daughter)

Grand Opening Day Saturday 14th July!

The 'Big' Day

It was the opening day at Micro World. Macro Marvel spoke to the happy crowd.

"Welcome to Micro World, the best theme park on earth. Micro World is micro-sized. You need to shrink to get in!"

Someone in the crowd called out, "Is it safe?"
"Do not be afraid," said Marvel. "I will go into the park first and send a signal for you to follow. Read this leaflet. It should explain everything."

Welcome to
MicroWorld

You need to shrink to get in!

5

Micro World

Your safety is important to us. Please read the information below.

Please stand on the conveyor belt to go into Micro World. The belt will go past the Shrinker. The Shrinker will make you small so you can get into the park. You will be made big again before you leave.

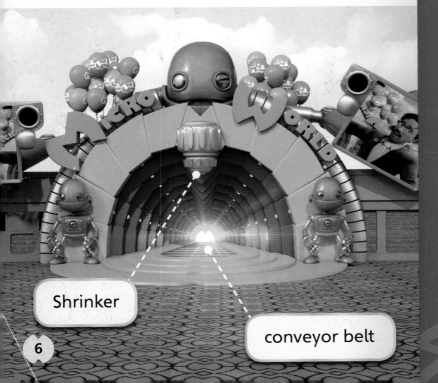

Shrinker

conveyor belt

There are 12 zones in Micro World.

The zones have different rides.

You must leave the zone by the exit doors. Then you can enter the next zone.

MITEs

These are MITEs. You will see them in the park. They are robots that look after the zones.

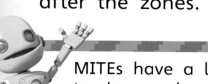

MITEs have a lot to do, so please do not try to play with them.

BITEs

These are BITEs. These robots make sure that the MITEs are doing their jobs. BITEs are harder to spot. There is a different BITE in each zone. They have red eyes when they are angry.

Please do not go near the BITEs.

Computer **O**perated **D**igital **E**ntity

A computer called CODE controls Micro World and all the robots in it.

CODE follows one rule: keep people safe.

The Shrinker

Everyone watched as Macro Marvel entered Micro World. He stood on the conveyor belt, and it started to move. As Marvel passed under the Shrinker, he shrank to micro-size. The crowd cheered as he entered the park.

The crowd waited and waited for the signal from Macro Marvel. Mini started to feel nervous. At last she got a message from her dad. 'STOP CODE!' was all it said.

Mini cried out, "Oh, no! Something has gone wrong."

Suddenly a huge eye appeared on the screen in front of them. It was CODE! The crowd fell silent as CODE spoke.

"Keep people safe. Make people small," said CODE. "There are too many people on the planet. There is too little food and too much pollution. I must make people small. Then they will not need so much food. Then they will not make so much pollution ..."

This is a massive micro emergency! WE NEED HELP!

Watch out! Shrinking rays!

CODE to Shrink Millions...

"We are getting reports that a massive surge of power has been detected at the new Micro World theme park. Soon a computer called CODE will have enough power to shoot shrinking rays around the earth. Millions of people will be made micro-size."

"Only Macro Marvel knows how to deactivate CODE, but he has not been seen since he entered the Shrinker earlier today. Marvel's daughter, Mini, went to try and find him. Neither of them have been seen since. Where are they? Can CODE be stopped? The world watches and waits ..."

Call for Team X

Far away, a warning signal flashed. Max, Cat, Ant and Tiger leaped into action.

Meet Team X, four kids with four amazing watches ... watches that allow them to shrink or grow to any size they want. Team X fights to save the world from danger.

Dani Day
(in charge of Team X)

Team X profiles

Name: Max
Age: 11

Likes: sport, reading and inventing things

Profile: kind, popular, Team X leader

climbing wire

force shield

hologram communicator

Name: Cat
Age: 11

Likes: football and music

Profile: clever, kind, fearless

Team X tracking device

magni-beam

Name: Ant
Age: 9

Likes: science and nature, loves animals

Profile: clever, good at solving problems

internet access

flip-up camera

Name: Tiger
Age: 10

Likes: football and adventures

Profile: funny, brave, can get into scrapes

climbing wire

warning light

torch

New Cool Kit

Okay, Team X, here is your special kit for this mission.

Jet Pack
Helps you shoot up and away.

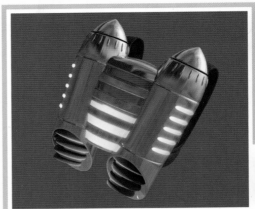
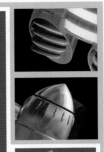

Bounce Boots
Go twice as far, twice as high!

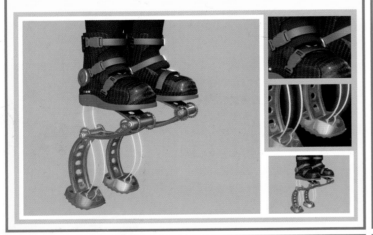

X-ray Glasses
Can look through any material.

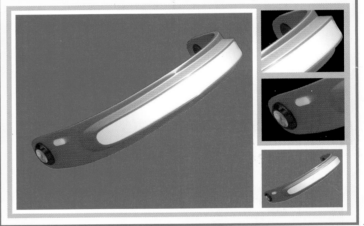

Power Mitts
Give you super strength when you need it most!

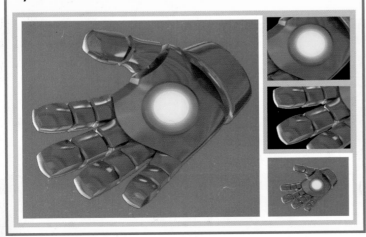

Sea Speeder
An underwater jet that pulls you along in the water.

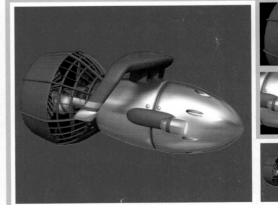
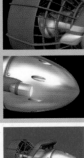

X-craft

Grass Chopper

Travels: over land

Speed:

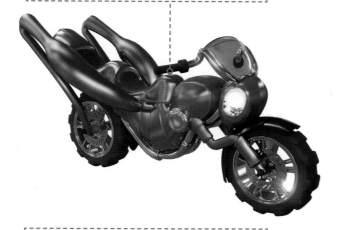

Driller

Travels: over land and underground

Speed:

Hawkwing

Travels: in air

Speed:

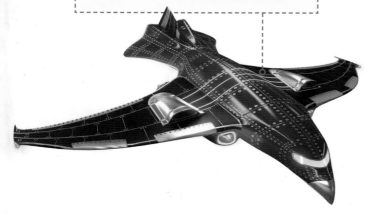

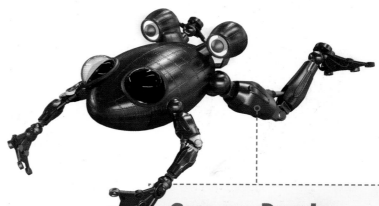

Green Dart

Travels: over land and underwater

Speed:

Bee-machine

Travels: in air

Speed:

To Micro World!

Team X grabbed their new kit. They jumped into the
Green Dart, their jet-powered craft. Cat switched on
the engine, and soon they were off to Marvel Island
and to Micro World!

When they reached the island, Team X climbed out of the Green Dart. Together they shrank it. Instantly, the Green Dart was micro-size.

Let's get to the park!

19

Past the Shrinker

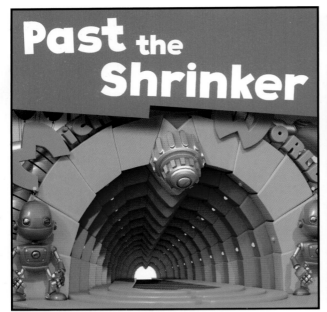

How do we get past the Shrinker?

Look at this place!

Wow!

"Need a little help?"

"Need a little help?" said a voice behind them. Team X spun around to see Mini standing there. She looked scared, but she was trying to smile. "Hi, I'm Mini Marvel. I can help you find your way through the theme park."

"There is a different BITE in each zone. Each one protects a CODE key. You need to battle the BITE and get the CODE key. Then you can unlock the exit door and get to the next zone. In the middle of the park you will find CODE. I think my dad will be there too. It will be dangerous. Oh, just one more thing, you're going to need me to come with you ..."

The New Mission

Together they have to:

- Defeat the BITEs
- Collect the CODE keys
- Rescue Macro Marvel
- Stop CODE
- Save the world!